THE COUGAR

THE BIG CAT DISCOVERY LIBRARY

Lynn M. Stone

Rourke Enterprises, Inc.
Vero Beach, Florida 32964

PHOTO CREDITS
© Tom and Pat Leeson: Pages: 1, 10, 15; © E. R. Degginger/
Animals Animals: Pages 12-13; © Lynn M. Stone: Pages 4, 7,
8, 17, 18, 21, and cover

ACKNOWLEDGEMENTS

The author wishes to thank the following for special
photographic assistance in the preparation of this book:
Catherine Hilker and the Cincinnati Zoo; Peter Caron and
Octagon Wildlife, North Fort Myers, Florida

Library of Congress Cataloging-in-Publication Date
Stone, Lynn M.
    Cougars / Lynn M. Stone.
    p. cm. — (The big cat discovery library)
    Includes index.
    Summary: An introduction to the physical characteristics,
habits, natural environment, relationship to humans, and future
of the cougar, a cat that is found in both North and South
America and known by at least five other names, includng
puma, catamount, painter, mountain lion, and panther.
    ISBN 0-86592-505-4
    1. Pumas—Juvenile literature [1. Pumas.] I. Title.
II. Series: Stone, Lynn M. Big cat discovery library.
QL737.C23S766 1989   89-32645
599.74'428—dc20   CIP
                                   AC

TABLE OF CONTENTS

THE COUGAR

Which **mammal** lives in more parts of North and South America than any other? That question has at least six right answers: cougar, catamount, painter, mountain lion, puma, and panther. All those names refer to the same big cat.

The cougar *(Felis concolor)* has the biggest range of any American mammal, and it probably has the biggest list of common names, too. One of them—mountain lion—came about because the tan cat was mistaken for an African lion. Dutch settlers in New York 350 years ago thought the cougar was the same as the lion of Africa. And explorers Amerigo Vespucci and Christopher Columbus both wrote of "lions" they had seen in North America.

Cougar

THE COUGAR'S COUSINS

The cougar is a **feline**, a member of the cat family. It has the typical fangs, claws, short jaws, and graceful movements of all cats.

The cougar's size would seem to make it a first cousin of other large, heavy cats. In fact, the cougar is quite different from jaguars, leopards, tigers, and lions. The cougar, for instance, can not roar. The other large cats can. But a cougar purrs like a house cat. The voice boxes of the other big cats are for roaring rather than purring.

Among all the cougars of the Americas are several slightly different groups. Cougars in South America are usually smaller and darker than the groups in North America.

The cougars in Florida, known as Florida panthers, are almost **extinct**.

Florida Panther

HOW THEY LOOK

Cougars have small heads and long necks attached to big, low-slung bodies. They have long, thick tails. The tail may help the cougar balance when it climbs or leaps.

Cougar fur is generally some shade of brown or gray with white underneath. Cougars in Canada and the northern United States have thicker fur than their cousins in South America.

Male cougars average 160 pounds. Females weigh 90 to 135 pounds. The largest cougar on record weighed 276 pounds!

Because of their color, cougars do resemble female lions. Cougars are much smaller, however. Among other things, they also lack the lion's broad head.

WHERE THEY LIVE

The cougar's range extends from northern Canada (south of the Arctic) south through the United States, Central America, and into Argentina. Most of the North American cougars are found in Alberta, British Columbia, the Rocky Mountain states, Texas, New Mexico, and the mountains of California, Oregon, and Washington.

Cougars are rare in the East. A few live in eastern Canada and in the southern half of Florida. Sometimes there are reports of cougars in northern New England, northern New York, and the Southern Appalachian Mountains.

The cougar's home, or **habitat**, within its huge range can be forest, brushland, grassland, or **semi-desert**. Florida cougars live at sea level. Cougars have also been found in the South American mountains as high as 14,800 feet above sea level!

Cougar in Mountain Meadow

Cougar with Prey in Desert

HOW THEY LIVE

Cougars lead very private lives. They are **nocturnal**, doing most of their hunting at night. They try to avoid people, and they usually avoid each other.

Cougars have home **territories** like many other cats. A cougar marks the edges of its territory with claw marks on trees and urine.

Cougars have fine hearing and eyesight, and a good sense of smell.

Thanks to long hind legs, cougars can jump extremely well. They are expert climbers, too. They can swim, but they dislike water.

Cougars roam great distances, especially at night. During the day they usually hide unless **prey**, the animals they eat, is scarce. Then they may be forced to hunt in daylight.

Cougar

THE COUGAR'S CUBS

A mother cougar usually has three or four spotted kittens, or cubs. They are born blind in a cave or some other hiding place.

Their eyes open in about two weeks. At six weeks, they may be taken by their mother to one of her kills.

The spots disappear late during the kittens' first year. By the age of 20 to 22 months, they have learned to **stalk** and kill their own prey. At this time they leave their mother and set up their own territories.

Cougars can live to age 11 or older.

Cougar Kitten

PREDATOR AND PREY

The cougar's range in the Americas is similar to the range of deer. Cougars are **predators**, or hunters. They will eat almost any animal they can catch, but deer are a favorite prey. A cougar hides its deer kills and returns to them for several meals.

Cougars stalk prey by moving very slowly toward an animal and crouching. When the cougar is close to its prey, it bounds from hiding and leaps upon it.

A cougar has the strength and teeth to kill a healthy elk or moose up to seven times its size. More often, it attacks young or ill animals.

Cougar Prey: Whitetail Deer

COUGARS AND PEOPLE

People have feared, hated and even loved cougars. The native people of the Americas have generally respected cougars. A city in Peru was built in a cougar's outline. The Cherokee Indians said the cougar was the greatest of wild hunters.

Settlers from Europe, however, viewed cougars as a danger to themselves and their animals. In 1694 Connecticut paid people for killing cougars. Other colonies did the same. These payments, called bounties, continued in some Western states through the 1960s!

Cougars are now completely protected by law in many states. In others they are "big game" animals and can only be hunted during certain seasons.

Cougars rarely kill farm animals, and they are almost never a threat to people.

"Florida Panther" on Stalk

THE COUGAR'S FUTURE

Ninety years ago President Theodore Roosevelt wrote that he was no more afraid of forests with cougars than he was of forests with tomcats. Many people in cougar country feel the same way. They are glad just to know the big cats are out there in the wilderness. Of course, when wilderness disappears, so do cougars.

Cougars are not really common anywhere. But with protection by man, their numbers could increase in some of their North American habitats.

No one knows for sure whether the cougar can make a comeback in the East. In Florida, where the panther is the state mammal, there are just 30 or so left. The last panther may be gone by the year 2000.

Glossary

extinct (ex TINKT)—no longer existing

feline (FEE line)—any of the cats

habitat (HAB a tat)—the area in which an animal lives

mammal (MAA mull)—a group of four-footed animals which produce milk and have either fur or hair

nocturnal (nok TUR nal)—active at night

predator (PRED a tor)—an animal that kills other animals for food

prey (PREY)—an animal that is hunted by another for food

semi-desert (SEMI DEZ ert)—an area similar to a true desert but not as dry

stalk (STAWK)—hunting by moving slowly and quietly toward prey

territory (TER rih tory)—a home area defended by certain animals that live within it

INDEX